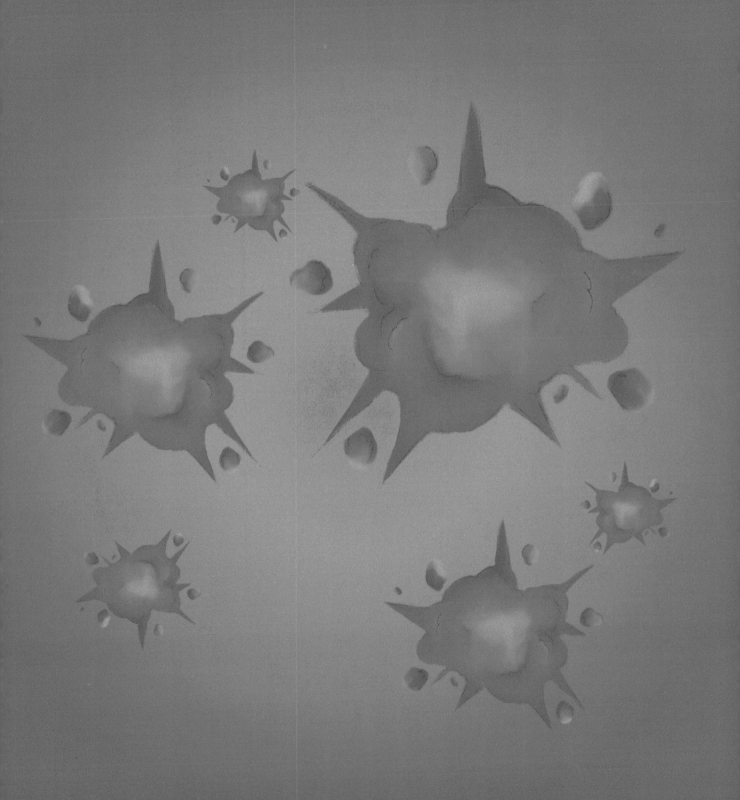

'FOR ALL THE DOERS WHO KNOW WHAT IT'S LIKE TO FEEL ANGRY BECAUSE OF MANY REASONS. WE NEED YOUR PASSION AND IDEAS IN THIS WORLD'

'Go-go Felt Angry' by Amanda Cox 2022
Illustrations by Mim Zariffa 2022
Digital Illustrations by Sarah Cox 2022

[1st Edition 2022, hard cover.]

ISBN: 978-0-6450250-7-1

Publishing services by: IngramSpark

Illustrations created by pencil
Digital illustrations created on Procreate and Adobe Photoshop

Disclaimer
This book contains principles and lessons from the author's lived experience and does not represent professional advice. For application to you or your child's specific circumstances, please seek counsel from your local community and/or health professional/s.

A catalogue record for this book is available from the National Library of Australia.

Go-go was **ANGRY**.

Everyone knew it.

Go-go had not been chosen to be the leader
and it was annoying. Go-go's hooves stamped the carpet
and Go-go began to argue with Mrs Llama.

At lunchtime, Go-go's friends didn't choose the
game Go-go wanted to play. They also hadn't agreed that
Go-go's idea for the upcoming school project was the
very best one, which Go-go thought was obvious AND
they lost at soccer!!

1+2=3

are special

Mrs Llama was trying to get Go-go to calmly talk to her,
she kept asking Go-go to stop yelling and stomping, and
this just made things worse.

Cookie, who was usually happy and laughing moved away quietly, Ginger was staring and Lop was nowhere to be found (Lop had probably moved to a quiet safe space. Lop really didn't like yelling).

Eventually, Go-go had to leave the classroom
to calm down. On the way out, Go-go was so upset,
that it seemed all of a sudden the big elm tree jumped
right in front of Go-go who bumped head
first into its thick unforgiving trunk.

Now Go-go's head hurt and Go-go started to cry.

It was a loud kind
of angry cry and
everyone found it
hard not to look
out the window,
and especially hard
to concentrate on
their school work.

Cookie felt **sad**.

Go-go often seemed LOUD and *bossy* but Cookie
knew that Go-go really didn't mean to be.
Go-go did have good ideas, was always busy,
really liked to be the winner and the leader,
always got bored but was a lot of fun to be around.

Often the others thought Go-go was rude and blunt and
when Go-go was not happy everyone knew about it!

Go-go often ended up in trouble. Just like now.

Cookie remembered how friends had helped when Cookie felt sad and began to wonder how to help Go-go feel better.

Cookie waited until
Go-go came back
inside before
asking if
Go-go would
like to hear a joke.

dad
jokes

Go-go was still a bit grumpy
but Cookie told one anyway…

Go-go tried not to laugh,

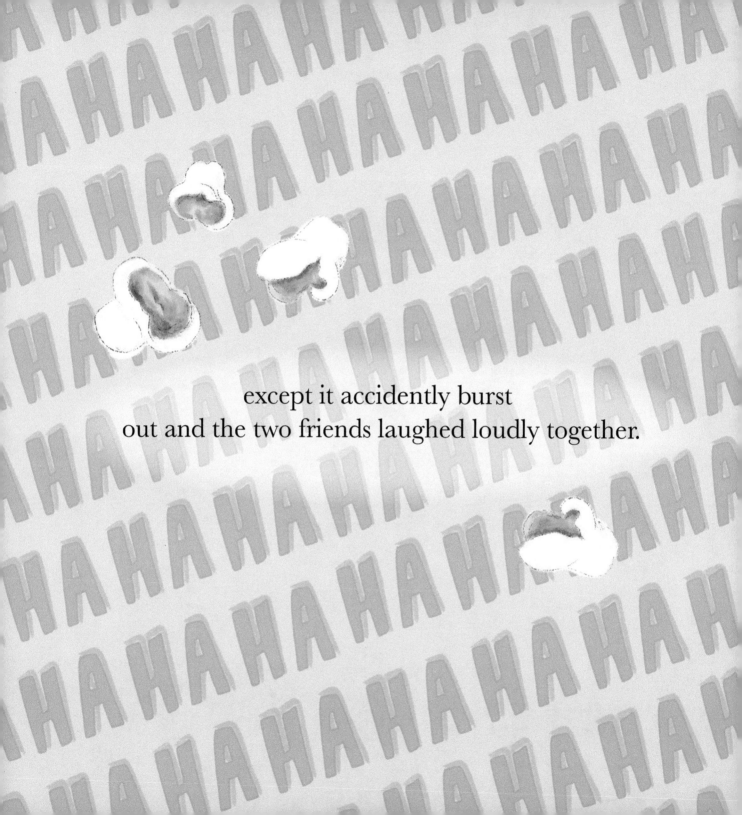

except it accidently burst
out and the two friends laughed loudly together.

Cookie asked if Go-go was ok.
It turned out Go-go didn't like being angry because it
made others feel sad.

Cookie understood but reminded
Go-go that being angry wasn't who Go-go was.
'Remember, Mrs Llama, says we are not how we feel.'

Go-go was learning that being angry
meant that Go-go also felt something else with
the anger and it was good to talk about this with
someone who is caring.

It was true Go-go felt angry more than the others, but they all looked different when they felt sad.

Go-go, Cookie, Lop and Ginger are learning we often all express our feelings differently, but it doesn't change WHO we truly are.

The truth is we are all

loved & SPECIAL.

Dear Parent, Grand-Parent, Teacher, Adult,

'Go-go Felt Angry' is one of four in a series of children's books. This series is specifically designed to help children understand and embrace their uniqueness. They are also written to invite discovery and acceptance of the differences in one another. The stories reflect varied perspectives and the individual ways we receive and respond to the world around us. Our first book, 'Cookie Felt Sad', highlighted some of the things that can be experienced when we fear disapproval. Lop, on the other hand, didn't find it easy to understand or express emotions and Ginger felt nervous about taking on responsibility. You've just read how Go-go responded to not being recognised. Our stories highlight how the characters have different ways of coping when we face things that are uniquely challenging to us.

Embracing and celebrating how we can all work together amid our individuality, is an important part of being in community. These stories are written with the heart to foster and create a space like this. We hope that our characters and their stories engage the young reader in identifying some of the ways that makes them wonderfully unique and maybe even create healthy wholesome discussions.

Creating a safe space to be accepted, understood and to be able to safely process out loud, helps to regulate emotions. This is a great way to nurture emotional and mental well-being. To support you in creating this space, we have included some discovery questions that you may find useful. We hope this is helpful for you and your young reader, and fosters an environment in which you can openly share with each other. A hot tip we have is to avoid trying to offer suggestions or fix another person's pain or problem. We can learn so much from listening to understand, rather than listening to respond. There is so much healing power in simply being heard. We hope that as an adult, you too, can enjoy our stories, and that you find the messages and the characters engaging and thought provoking.

DISCOVERY QUESTIONS:

Have you ever been angry?

What sort of things make you feel really angry?

Do you like to be selected to be the leader?

What happens if people don't do what you want?
How do you feel about this? Why do you think that is?

Have people called you 'bossy' before?
How did this make you feel?

Amanda identifies with Go-go, and as an adult, has experienced great relief and freedom through learning about her uniqueness, as well as understanding more about her desire to be the boss. For many years, Amanda lived ashamed of her unique personal characteristics, but now she embraces them in creative and entrepreneurial ways to help and support others. She loves people and her heart beats wildly for empowering and equipping them to also understand and embrace their own uniqueness. Amanda is a testament to the fact when we live in a place of having a healthy identity, the things we are often ashamed of and hid from, become a launchpad for our own incredible unfolding story.

Mim discovered the world of creating with coloured pencil when relocating to Tasmania. Her love of art and psychology inspired her to follow her heart, and since then she has embraced this world by journeying alongside people and utilising her creativity.
This incredible talent is displayed in the engaging illustrations we see in the series of stories about our four very unique and differnt characters. It's been life-changing for Mim to learn about how beautifully unique each person is created. It's also helped her understand people with characteristics like Go-go, who in the past she foundintimidating, feeling that she needed to be more and do more in order to keep up with them.Appreciating her uniqueness has been the impetus for Mim to embrace her identity, and alsofoundational in inspiring others.

Sarah has always loved finding ways to creatively express herself. In more recent years she has been exploring her creative talent, through the use of technology, and continually learning about all the different ways this can be used to enhance and improve her ever-broading skill set. She's also found through her own life's journey, a passion for understanding one's uniqueness and the importance of children understanding this too as they grow up and experience life. Sarah can relate a lot to Go-go in her uniqueness. For a lot of her life she's tried to suppress the characteristics of Go-go because she thought it made her look bad, and would mean she wouldn't be accepted. However, it's only been in recent years, that's she's been learning to embrace these parts of herself and allow herself to see the beauty in what is her uniqueness.

Go-go Felt Angry' is the final book in our series, and like the other stories, it's unique in its own way (that's the whole idea behind this series). In creating the storyline for this book, we would like to acknowledge and honour the budding young leaders and authors who contributed to it. This group of fabulous students were brave and open and honest about their experience of leadership as well as their thoughts on feeling angry when things don't go their way. Together, we had so much fun workshopping a story line. We are in admiration of their big smiles, soft hearts and creative ideas.

Go-go felt angry is the last of a series of four children's books. Each book features temperament characteristics of the character. The heart of these stories is to inspire and encourage young readers that we are all unique. It is our hope that young and old readers alike, might identify with some of these characteristics along the way and lean into understanding the diverse way we receive and react to the world and people around us.

There are several treasures to be discovered hidden within the stories. These are included to inspire ongoing conversations about healthy mental and emotional wellbeing. More information about these can be found at www.findingspace.com.au on the 'hidden treasures' tab within our children's book page.

CPSIA information can be obtained
at www.ICGtesting.com
Printed in the USA
LVHW071908200922
728861LV00010B/156